THE
LOS ANGELES
RIOTS

America's Cities in Crisis

John Salak

THE MILLBROOK PRESS
Brookfield, Connecticut

Published by The Millbrook Press
2 Old New Milford Road
Brookfield, CT 06804
© 1993 Blackbirch Graphics, Inc.
First Edition

5 4 3 2 1

Created and produced in association with Blackbirch Graphics.
Series Editor: Bruce S. Glassman

Library of Congress Cataloging-in-Publication Data
Salak, John
      The Los Angeles Riots: America's cities in crisis / John Salak.
      Includes bibliographical references and index.
      Summary: Surveys the background and causes of urban unrest in
America and describes the 1992 riots in Los Angeles and their aftermath.
      1. Los Angeles (Calif.)—Race relations—Juvenile literature. 2. Afro-
Americans—California—Los Angeles—Social conditions—Juvenile
literature. 3. Riots—California—Los Angeles—History—20th century—
Juvenile literature. 4. Urban policy—United States—Juvenile literature.
[1. Riots—California—Los Angeles. 2. Los Angeles (Calif.)—Race
relations. 3. Race relations.] I. Title. II. Series.
ISBN 1-56294-373-1 (lib. bdg.)
F869.L89N369 1993
979.4'9400496073—dc20   92-30572
                                                                     CIP
                                                                      AC

Contents

Chapter One/ A Spark Ignites a Flame 5

Chapter Two/ America's Turbulent Past 13

Chapter Three/ Anatomy of a Riot 23

Chapter Four/ The Aftermath 43

Chapter Five/ Healing the Wounds 53

Chronology 61

For Further Reading 61

Index 62

Chapter *1*

A Spark Ignites a Flame

L ate in the afternoon on April 29, 1992, a jury in
Ventura County, California, acquitted four white
Los Angeles police officers of assaulting Rodney
King, a black man, during an arrest. It was a verdict that
did much more than find four police officers not guilty.
It caused a social explosion that rocked Los Angeles and
was felt in every city, town, and suburb in the United States.

The twenty-nine day trial had captivated the country
and the world. Even before the first witness testified, the
case received enormous attention not only because of the
underlying possibilities of racism and police brutality, but
because the arrest and beating had been videotaped and
shown repeatedly on television for months. It seemed to
be an open-and-shut case.

The surprise was obvious as soon as the first "not
guilty" verdict was read. The courtroom erupted. Sup-
porters of the police officers shouted their relief, while
others who thought they were guilty screamed in rage.

Tensions continued to mount on the courthouse steps
as the freed officers had to be protected from a violent
crowd that gathered. The anger, however, did not subside
as the police officers drove away. It only grew, particularly
in the city's poor black and Hispanic neighborhoods, until

Rage over the
verdict in the
Rodney King
case exploded
on the streets
of Los Angeles.

Opposite:
Fires raged out of control
for days during the riots.

A Korean shop owner takes to the streets with a gun to protect himself and his business.

it became a spark that would set off the worst urban riots in America in twenty-five years. In the four days that followed, parts of Los Angeles became war zones that were out of police control.

The violence spilled out of Los Angeles's black and Hispanic neighborhoods, although they suffered extensively. It touched the entire city, the nation's second largest. Fires raged, buildings were leveled, and stores were looted. Property damage from the riots was estimated near $1 billion. The human cost was even greater, estimated at fifty-two deaths and countless numbers of injured people. Violence and rioting were also touched off in other cities across the nation.

The anger and destruction shocked the country. Americans, after all, had not seen large-scale riots in their cities since the 1960s. Since that time hundreds of programs and hundreds of billions of dollars had been spent to guarantee civil rights and improve conditions for America's urban poor. Now, however, with parts of Los Angeles in flames and unrest breaking out in other cities, the country was forced once again to look into its ghettos to understand why people, many of whom had been generally law-abiding, would take to the streets in droves to destroy, steal, and kill.

One black community leader offered this explanation. "A few weeks ago, I would have told black high-school students there was a justice system that would protect them. After the King verdict, I cannot tell them that they're not being discriminated against because they're black. I can't tell them that anymore, because I don't believe it anymore. It's horribly painful. It makes me want to weep."

The two areas hardest hit by the riots were both heavily Hispanic. According to some estimates, more than nine hundred Hispanic businesses were destroyed in the rioting.

Hispanic and Korean Communities Hit Hard

Many Korean businesses were targeted for looting. Witnessing the destruction of their livelihood, some store owners lost faith in the promise of the "American dream." "This is not America," said Korean immigrant Charles Kim, soon after his L.A. store was destroyed in the riot. "We are all brothers. Why are they doing this?" Among business owners, Koreans suffered the most. About 60 percent of the 4,000 business owners who reported damage to the L.A. police were Korean, according to the city's deputy mayor, Linda Griego.

The two areas worst hit by the riots were South Central Los Angeles and Koreatown, both heavily Hispanic. According to the 1990 census, 45 percent of South Central was Hispanic, as was 68 percent of Koreatown. Even though most media attention focused on Korean business

A clothing-store owner reacts to seeing her business go up in flames.

losses, estimates for damage to Hispanic enterprises were also high. "As far as we can determine," said Bert Corono, director of the immigrant assistance organization Hermandad Mexicana Nacional, "eight hundred to nine hundred Hispanic-owned businesses were partially or totally wiped out or had to relocate." Lucrecia Garcia, president of Unión de Comerciantes Latinos, estimated that the average loss of Hispanic small businesses was up-wards of $75,000 per business. In addition, many Hispanic aid agencies reported that a large percentage of the businesses that were affected were not covered by insurance.

The country soon discovered there were no simple answers to why people rioted. The reasons could not be limited to racism, poverty, and police brutality, although they all played a part. Finding ways to effectively battle the causes of urban unrest would prove no easier. Yet, even before the last fires were extinguished in Los Angeles, there was pressure for federal and local authorities to come up with programs to rebuild the inner cities and provide new hope for the people who live there. Despite these calls, changes did not come quickly. Understanding had to come first.

A Look at Urban Unrest

To fully understand the causes of urban unrest, the term has to be defined first. Urban unrest differs from street crime. Street crimes, such as robbery or mugging, involve individuals or people in small groups. These activities may be the result of large-scale social problems such as poverty, drug abuse, and inequality, but they remain incidents in which people harm others for specific, usually limited, reasons, such as getting money. Street crimes can happen anywhere, from small towns to suburbs to big cities.

Urban unrest is a much broader term and is, by definition, limited to cities. It involves the mass movement of a large portion of a city's population against society in

Protestors outside the
L.A.P.D. after the Rodney
King verdict were expressing
the outrage and disbelief felt
by many people across the
country.

general. Urban unrest may appear to be a reaction to a
specific incident—such as the Rodney King verdict—but it
is usually a response to long-standing, unresolved conflicts
between a given population and its system of government
or law enforcement. Urban unrest can include street
crimes, such as looting, mugging, and widespread gang
violence. It can also include large-scale destruction of
entire neighborhoods and rioting between large groups of
people. In simple terms, urban unrest is many citizens
acting out their anger and frustration together over the
way things are.

The anger and frustration that unite citizens in urban
unrest, however, often quickly split them apart. Individuals view the chaos generated by unrest as an opportunity
to further their own interests. As a result, looting or

large-scale stealing often takes place. During urban unrest, some express their rage by simply destroying property, whether it belongs to city government or someone living or working in the community. Society at large may be the cause of urban unrest, but in the end, it is society that usually winds up the victim.

Whatever the causes or consequences, urban unrest is not new. It has been a part of world history as long as there have been cities, and it has occurred in almost every country. In fact, many of history's most important events started out as riots. The storming of the Bastille Prison by a Paris mob in 1789 spearheaded the French Revolution. More recently, the fall of communism in the Soviet Union can be traced in part to the citizens of Moscow taking to the streets by the thousands to protest the illegal takeover of Mikhail Gorbachev's reformist government by Communist hard-liners in August 1991.

American cities haven't been immune to civil disturbances. Many of these incidents have played a significant role in shaping the country. They have reflected the social and political changes of their times. Ultimately, these changes and pressures helped to create a distinctly American form of urban unrest.

Chapter 2

America's Turbulent Past

The causes and consequences of urban unrest have
changed over the years. But riots have always
been part of America's urban culture. The nation's
first notable disturbances, in fact, predate the American
Revolution.

After almost two years of growing tensions between
British and colonial leaders, hundreds of colonial residents
took to the streets of Boston in April 1770 to protest the
Townshend Acts that forced them to house British troops.
What began as a simple protest turned into a riot when
people gathered and began taunting British soldiers,
crowding them into a corner. The violence escalated
when the mob started to hurl sticks and stones at the
troops, who eventually panicked and opened fire, killing
five people. The incident became known as the Boston
Massacre and was to become a rallying cry for the Americans throughout the Revolutionary War.

There is often only a fine line between a peaceful dem-
onstration and a riot, especially when many people with
underlying tensions and conflicting aims gather. In 1886,
at Chicago's Haymarket Square, 1,500 workers peacefully
demonstrating for shorter workdays (eight hours) found
out how easy it is to cross that line. No one was sure who

Long-standing
social problems
and inequality
have fueled
many riots in
our cities.

Opposite:
One of America's earliest
riots was in 1770, when
citizens took to the streets
of Boston to protest the
Townshend Acts.

Civil War Draft Riots

Riots are rarely explained easily. They are often the product of rising frustrations that develop for many reasons. The worst riot in American history is a prime example of how several factors can combine to create a riot. Surprisingly, it didn't occur in an overcrowded twentieth-century city, but rather in Manhattan almost 130 years ago. There, in July 1863, at the height of the Civil War, new draft laws forcing men into the army served as the cause of four days of unprecedented urban violence. It was a disaster that rose from political, economic, and social pressures.

The rioters were mainly Irish immigrants who lived in poverty in the overcrowded and disease-ridden tenements of lower Manhattan. The Irish were generally not in favor of the war, fearing that the emancipation of the slaves would mean free black men rushing to the North to take away jobs. Naturally, the Irish didn't like the new draft laws because these laws forced them to fight in a war they didn't support. The Irish also believed the new laws were unfair. Poor people, like them, were made to go into the army, while the wealthy could avoid the fighting by paying for substitutes. The beginning of the draft alone might have been enough to push these Irishmen to riot. However, their anger was encouraged by Democratic politicians who were out to hurt the war aims of President Abraham Lincoln's Republican Party.

The politicians stirred up the emotions of the immigrants in many ways. For example, shortly before the uprising, the editor of the city's leading Catholic newspaper, which had strong ties to both the Irish and the Democrats, challenged the president's authority. He told a mass meeting of largely Irish immigrants that when the president called on them to go and carry on a war for the slaves, he would "be damned if he believed they would go."

The resentment of these immigrants exploded into a full-scaie riot after draft officers appeared in New York to sign up recruits. Roaming Irish immigrants attacked people and buildings throughout New York for four days. Black men and women were particular targets, as were federal offices and buildings and companies that employed blacks. By the time the rioting had ended, at least 105 people were dead and more than a thousand were injured.

sparked the violence. But it began when a bomb exploded as police officers moved in to control the crowd. In the end, the Haymarket Square riot left eleven people dead and hundreds hurt.

America is a country of many ethnic groups. Tensions between groups have always existed. In fact, they have usually grown as newcomers crowd into cities and seem to threaten the prosperity of those people who are already there. Rarely, however, did this uneasy peace result in riots. That began to change with the approach of the twentieth century, as larger-than-ever numbers of immigrants poured into the country, usually into already overcrowded cities, where living conditions were tough. In 1891, these frictions led to riots in New Orleans, when rumors spread that Italian immigrants were responsible for killing a local police superintendent. Several Italians were arrested, but they were later cleared of the charges. Nonetheless, a mob of 20,000 people—spurred on by local politicians—rioted and eventually stormed a police station and killed eleven Italian immigrants who were in protective custody.

Conflict in the Twentieth Century

Rioting in American cities did not ease with the twentieth century. In some ways, it only grew more intense as the country faced new challenges despite its growing wealth. Again, race played a large part. New tensions between ethnic groups occurred in part because people began moving around the country following World War I. One

The Haymarket riot of 1886 began as a peaceful protest by Chicago workers for a shorter workday.

In 1965, race riots in Los Angeles's Watts neighborhood left 34 dead and $440 million in property damage.

major shift involved blacks who were leaving farms in the South to move to northern cities, such as Detroit, Cleveland, Chicago, and New York. With this influx of blacks, many of these northern cities had to deal with the issue of race relations for the first time. Until then, it had always been a "southern problem."

While blacks may have left the farms of the South in search of a better life, they rarely found it. Living conditions in northern cities were usually bad. Blacks often were forced into squalid and overcrowded apartment buildings. They were paid less than whites, they received less schooling and health care, and they suffered higher unemployment. Often they were blocked from having a political voice or improving their standard of living by moving up the social ladder. Naturally this bred frustrations. By the 1950s, the civil rights movement was working to change this. Improvements were made, particularly in the first half of the 1960s, when federal legislation ensuring voting and civil rights was passed.

Despite these changes, frustration was rising in black communities. Improvements had raised the expectations of the urban poor. Yet changes weren't coming fast enough. The growing power of television, which emphasized the material wealth of the nation, only helped to fuel the anger of people who wanted more but could not get it. The resentment among inner-city blacks was particularly strong. Black unemployment in the early 1960s was twice as high as white unemployment. And the differences in living conditions and wages between the races were widening.

By the summer of 1965, these pressures brought tensions in the inner cities to a boiling point. They also made the name *Watts* symbolic of a new wave of urban unrest. In this L.A. neighborhood, not far from the site of the 1992 riots, the arrest of a black man by white police sparked three days of rioting and looting. Much of the anger was directed at whites and white-owned businesses in the neighborhood. In the end, 34 people died, 1,032 were injured, 3,775 were arrested, and $440 million in property was damaged. Yet the rioting that began in Watts didn't end there. Television helped to spread the news and images, which some said encouraged outbreaks elsewhere. The following year, riots erupted in forty-three cities, including Omaha, Chicago, Cleveland, Atlanta, and San Francisco. The summer of 1967 brought new and more severe disturbances. The assassination of beloved civil rights leader Martin Luther King, Jr., intensified the rage and frustration felt by many in America's urban

Jacob Riis was an early social reformer who examined the living conditions in America's inner cities in an attempt to decrease social unrest.

communities. Detroit and Newark suffered the most that summer. In the three years that followed Watts, more than one hundred inner-city riots occurred. The toll was enormous: 225 dead, four thousand wounded, and hundreds of millions of dollars worth of property damaged.

Many of the factors that have led to American riots during the last two centuries are similar to those faced by cities around the world. Living conditions in crowded ghettos and low-paying jobs are among the main reasons people have expressed their discontent. Police brutality, political repression, and economic and social problems have also spurred riots here and elsewhere. They are probably the underlying reasons for rioting in this century and have virtually touched every group in the United States.

Any country can have problems with racism and discrimination. But discrimination has always been a significant element of American culture because of the country's history as a melting pot—a place made up of many different immigrants mixing together. Today, the mixing continues. Instead of waves of European immigrants pouring in, however, newcomers now arrive from places such as Vietnam, Korea, Taiwan, the Caribbean, and South America. As in the past, this latest mixing has not always gone smoothly.

American cities face increasingly complex social problems that go beyond the traditional factors of racism, social injustice, and economic hardships. These factors include the rise of inner-city gangs and the increased availability of powerful automatic weapons. Here is an instance in which street crime—such as gang warfare—has escalated urban unrest and in some cases made the violence more deadly than ever. In the past twenty years, there has also been a breakdown of the social fabric of many communities, which has helped to destabilize life in the ghettos. The number of one-parent families is rising. Drug addiction is on the increase, as is homelessness.

There are indications, too, that churches and other social-support groups have lost influence in their communities. Economic conditions in many cities have also worsened for the poor and semi-skilled.

Reform

While riots have increased in America, so have efforts to solve the problems of the poor that lead to violence. This has been especially true since the late 1890s, when a new wave of reformers began examining conditions in the ghettos, which were becoming increasingly crowded as more immigrants arrived. Jacob Riis, an early activist, helped to form laws regulating conditions in tenements. Others supported new laws on education, medical care, and child and adult labor.

The measures helped to decrease social unrest, but only to a limited extent. Those who were locked into the harsh conditions of inner-city life soon realized that the only sure way they were going to improve their lives was to save enough money to get out. Once people left, there was little reason to work on improving conditions in the ghettos.

The success of the reform efforts also depended on whether activists could maintain enough national interest to pay for their plans. They discovered that the momentum behind their efforts could easily disappear, especially when the nation's attention and resources were drawn elsewhere.

As the twentieth century progressed, the Great Depression of the 1930s and World War II created national emergencies that demanded enormous effort. They left little money or energy for dealing with urban problems. By the middle of the 1950s, however, the growing civil rights movement also began to foster new efforts to improve conditions in the inner cities, both in economic and social terms.

The Kerner Report

Lyndon Johnson's Great Society program was designed to help America's poor.

The riots of the 1960s left the country confused. While no one pretended that President Johnson's Great Society had eliminated the problems of the inner cities, conditions had certainly improved, and the federal government had poured millions of dollars into helping the country's poor and fighting racism and social injustices.

President Johnson established the Kerner Commission to investigate the rioting. The commission presented a startling conclusion. It warned that two Americas were forming. One was white and affluent, the other black and disadvantaged. Despite the reforms, it reported that racial differences were actually increasing. And the more they increased, the more the chance for urban disturbances increased.

Surprisingly, the programs of the Great Society and the civil rights movement were actually adding to the frustrations of blacks. The commission told the country what many blacks already understood. Changes were coming but not fast enough to meet these new expectations.

The rate of change began to accelerate. Significant federal reforms began in the 1960s during the administrations of Presidents John F. Kennedy and Lyndon B. Johnson. They culminated in President Johnson's Great Society. This was an agenda of sweeping reforms and new efforts. Among other things, it would ensure civil and voting rights to all Americans and provide the poor with economic aid, low-cost housing, health care, and job training.

President Johnson was successful in getting many of his programs passed. Questions remain, however, about whether his program was successful in helping the poor over the long run. In any event, his efforts began to falter as the country's attention and resources turned to the Vietnam War. Eventually, the political and economic demands of this Asian conflict made it difficult for President Johnson to get the remainder of his Great Society program in place.

The 1970s and 1980s

Efforts to improve conditions continued. But, as the memories of unrest, such as Watts, faded, the urgency seemed to wane as well.

In 1977, the Carter administration, for example, tried to set up several new programs, such as Urban Development Action Grants. These grants were designed to bring private and public funds together to develop the urban projects. The success of the grants, however, was limited because of inadequate funding.

By the late 1970s, the country was becoming more conservative and, in some ways, less concerned about the poor. People, in general, were more worried about battling crime and drugs in their own neighborhoods than in the ghettos. At the same time, there seemed to be a growing consensus that perhaps too much aid was going to the poor without demands that the poor work for themselves. These changes didn't help conditions in the ghettos—conditions that were growing worse and would lead to another explosion.

CONTINUED
CLAIMS

CLAIMS COUNTER HOURS
8:00 AM - 10:00 AM

MON - TUES - WED

Chapter 3

Anatomy of a Riot

The 1990s put new burdens on American cities and the people who lived there. After a decade of incredible economic growth, the country began to slip into a deep economic recession. Conditions worsened everywhere for all segments of the population. Yet people in the inner cities and minority groups, who were suffering before the recession began, were hit particularly hard by the economic downturn.

This was especially true of South Central Los Angeles, a depressed 46-square-mile area that is home to a large number of blacks, Hispanics, and Asian Americans.

Los Angeles was suffering through its worst recession since the end of World War II. Economic conditions in the city's ghettos were even more depressed. Heavy manufacturing companies, such as Southwest Steel, Chrysler, Firestone, and Goodyear, had left the region in recent years, taking hundreds of thousands of jobs with them. Companies that ventured into the area, often through government incentive programs, did not offset the losses of past wages and jobs; they often offered lower-paying jobs as an alternative. As a result, on the eve of the riots, unemployment among black, Hispanic, and Asian men between the ages of 18 and 35 was running at almost

A failing economy and rising unemployment added to the frustration and anger in already struggling neighborhoods.

Opposite:
A severe economic recession in the early 1990s put an even greater strain on Los Angeles's poorest areas.

50 percent. The average household income in the south central area was about $20,000, one third less than the average for the whole of Los Angeles.

The deterioration of the local job market created a growing despair in the area, according to some analysts. It led many of the chronically unemployed to give up on trying to find jobs or improve their living conditions.

Rising drug use, street crime, and homelessness also helped to destabilize the area. In addition, gang member-

Long-standing tensions between minorities and police fueled resentment in many quarters of South Central Los Angeles.

ship and violence grew. Gang involvement in the drug trade gave members access to large amounts of money to purchase an increasingly sophisticated arsenal of weapons. This power led to regular gun battles with police and rival gangs.

Support structures, such as extended families, churches, and social groups, also began to break down. In 1960, for example, only 10 percent of black children nationwide lived in single-parent homes. By 1989, that figure had jumped to 53 percent, and it was probably even higher as 1992 began, especially in South Central Los Angeles. The number of single-parent families among various Hispanic groups was lower, at about 30.5 percent. This compares with 17 percent of the nation as a whole.

The strength and influence of local minority politicians and community leaders also seemed to be slipping.

Against this background of deteriorating social and economic conditions, tensions between the city's various ethnic groups had risen. The resentment between blacks and whites had a long and bitter history and had demonstrated itself in the riots of the 1960s. New frictions, however, began to surface in the 1980s between blacks and the rising number of Hispanic and Asian immigrants. Hispanics, in fact, are the largest minority group in the city, accounting for 40 percent of the total population. Asians now also make up a slightly larger portion of the city's population than do blacks—11 percent, compared with 10.5 percent.

The shift has resulted in new conflicts. Hispanics and blacks, either through gangs, economic groups, or on an individual level, found themselves fighting over the shrinking economic benefits of the inner city. Both groups, however, expressed rising resentment over the Asian immigrants, particularly Koreans, who have been more successful at establishing themselves in the United States by opening small businesses, often in the middle of predominantly black or Hispanic neighborhoods.

The Police and Minorities

Beyond the specific tensions between ethnic groups in Los Angeles was the long history of friction between minorities and city authorities across the nation. Perhaps the oldest and most significant is the tension between minority groups and the police. Black and Hispanic community leaders have long charged that police have systematically discriminated against them. They have pointed to a time during the 1970s when sixteen blacks died as police used chokeholds to subdue them during arrests or other incidents. At that time, L. A. police chief Daryl Gates angered minority leaders by claiming the procedure was an acceptable means of controlling a suspect. He even suggested that blacks might have a particular physical handicap that made them vulnerable to choking to death.

The issue of minority distrust of the police goes beyond the use of chokeholds. Before the verdict in the Rodney King case, police brutality against minorities was a recurrent national problem. In several earlier cases, police officers who were charged with beatings were acquitted, fueling resentment among minorities that police actions appeared to go beyond the law.

The tensions over the use of police force were not one-sided. Officers often felt that they were the victims. Their work, they argued, especially in the inner cities, was difficult and dangerous. When on patrol in the L. A. ghettos, an officer was under constant threat of physical attack and verbal abuse.

The police were also demoralized by complaints that their department was biased and inefficient. Many officers were confused over the public's demand for reforming their department, while at the same time wanting a stronger police presence on the streets to curb crime and the drug trade.

A report on the L. A. P. D. (Los Angeles Police Department) put out by James Q. Wilson, a UCLA professor and law-enforcement authority, underscored the problems for police and noted there were no simple solutions to the tensions facing officers. According to his report, the 8,000-member police force was understaffed by about 50 percent. This put enormous pressure on individual officers. In addition, the department's low morale hurt its efficiency. Finally, the department failed to maintain a working relationship with the city's various communities.

Leaders of Los Angeles's black and Hispanic communities charged that police officers systematically discriminated against the city's minorities.

The Catalyst

On March 3, 1991, a report of police brutality in Los Angeles shocked the entire nation. A twenty-five-year-old black construction worker named Rodney King had been severely beaten by four Los Angeles police officers. The entire incident, the details of which were gory and unbelievable, had been captured on videotape by a local resident.

Reports of the circumstances varied greatly from source to source. According to L.A. officials, the incident began when a highway-patrol unit spotted King's car speeding down San Fernando's Foothill Freeway at more than one hundred miles per hour. After a high-speed chase, King—who had other passengers in his Hyundai—was finally stopped. Police officers then allegedly asked King to get out of his car, which he did reluctantly. At that point, reports said, King—who was allegedly drunk— resisted an attempt by the officers to handcuff him. After knocking him to the ground, three of the officers began to kick and beat King while their sergeant looked on. Months later, a close inspection of the videotape revealed that King was clubbed and kicked a total of fifty-six times in eighty-one seconds. Some of those blows were dealt with a Taser gun, an electrical-shock device used by police to stun and subdue suspects.

Within hours, the graphic videotape of King's beating was being aired on national television. It was not long before the images and the story reached news agencies around the world, stirring international outrage. Americans throughout the nation expressed shock and disgust at what they saw. Mayor Tom Bradley ordered an immediate investigation, as protests and messages of outrage poured into Los Angeles from every region of the country.

The King beating rallied many Americans to denounce an injustice that appeared to be beyond question. After all, the "evil" and brutality were there on the videotape for

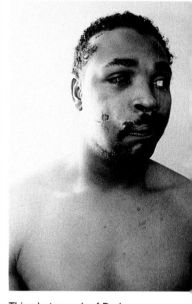

This photograph of Rodney King was taken three days after his videotaped beating. Among many injuries, King sustained a fractured skull and a fractured eye socket.

all to see, over and over again. The tape convinced many that racism was far from absent in America; Rodney King's battered and bloody face was testimony to that. If the beating had any positive side, many hoped, it would be that it could serve as harsh but undeniable proof of the serious race problems America still faced.

Questions of Fairness

The four white L.A.P.D. officers involved in the beating were Ted Briseno, Laurence Powell, Timothy Wind, and their sergeant, Stacey Koon. Under great pressure from a national public outcry, authorities promptly arrested the officers and brought them up on felony-assault charges. Once the indictments were handed down, however, it would be more than a year before their trial actually began.

As the months went by, Americans became more and more convinced of the officers' guilt. By the time the trial began, about 80 percent of blacks and whites believed the police were guilty. Most also had no doubt that the officers would be rightfully punished by the justice system.

By March of 1992, the judge and jury were selected, but not without more controversy. After rejecting two other locations for the proceedings, L.A. superior court judge Stanley Weisberg ordered the trial to be held in the

These frames were taken from the videotape of Rodney King's beating. After being aired for days on national television and across the world, the tape was viewed frame by frame by the jury in the case.

overwhelmingly white Ventura County community of
Simi Valley. Protests followed immediately. Not only was
Simi just 2 percent black (total population approximately
100,000), but it was also home to a large number of police
officers and firefighters. The apparent lack of fairness,
however, did not end there. Of the twelve-member jury,
ten members were white, one was Hispanic, and one was
Filipino. Not one African American was selected. Rang-
ing in age from thirty-eight to sixty-five, three of the
jurors had worked as security guards or patrol officers in
the military. Three others were members of the National
Rifle Association. One was the brother of a retired L.A.
police sergeant. Faced with this information, many citizens, both poor and well-to-do, experienced a serious
crisis of confidence in America's legal system. How could
any court allow things to appear so unfair?

The judge and jury heard testimony for twenty-nine
days, many of which were filled with continuous viewings
of the infamous videotape. A doctor testified to King's
injuries, describing fourteen separate medical conditions
that resulted from the beating. The doctor said that King
had suffered a fractured skull that might leave permanent
brain damage, a fractured right eye socket that caused
blurred vision, nerve damage that caused partial facial
paralysis, and multiple burns inflicted by electrical charges
from the Taser gun. Confident that the videotape and the
doctor's account would merely reinforce what appeared to
be an open-and-shut case, King's attorneys presented only
six witnesses during the twenty-nine days. Lawyers for the
defense, however, used a much more aggressive strategy.

To make their case, the defense lawyers showed the
videotape to the jury, repeating it frame by frame and in
slow motion. Their goal was to show that Rodney King
was, in fact, acting in a dangerous manner during the
beating. With each replay of the tape, lawyers called
attention to key moments and small details; each frame
showed, they said, that despite appearances, King was in

fact moving in a threatening way toward the four officers. The defense called a total of forty-nine witnesses, almost all of whom were police officers or experts on law enforcement. All claimed that the actions taken by the officers in the videotape fell within L.A.P.D. guidelines. By the time the defense lawyers concluded their arguments, they had convinced the jury that the officers had not broken the law. The jury came back with a "not guilty" verdict that cleared all four men of any wrongdoing.

A few hours after the King verdict was announced, the streets of South Central Los Angeles were ablaze.

The chaos that erupted in the courthouse when the verdict was read was only the beginning. In little more than an hour, residents of inner cities across America would react to the news with violent and uncontrolled rage. By nightfall, Los Angeles—the nation's second largest city—would be ablaze from a thousand fires.

The Riot—The Impact

The verdict caught everyone off guard, including the police. Well before the trial ended, Police Chief Daryl Gates reported that plans were in place to control any disturbances that might come about as a result of the trial. Yet it appeared that neither Gates nor his department expected the verdict, nor were they prepared to control the riots that followed.

The first disturbances came on the steps of the courthouse, where angry crowds shouted, "Guilty! Guilty! Guilty!" as the acquitted officers were led away. But the anger didn't end there.

Ninety minutes later, riots broke out elsewhere when crowds gathered at the intersection of Florence and Normandie streets in South Central Los Angeles—the heart of the inner city. A relatively small group of twenty-five officers tried to break up the crowd and made a few arrests. Yet the crowds began to overwhelm them. Shouts were followed by a barrage of rocks and bottles, and finally the crowds started swarming on the police. The police, outnumbered and without a coordinated plan of action, withdrew from the area to seek protection. At that point, the angry group of demonstrators turned into an uncontrolled mob of rioters.

The fires came first—as many as several dozen burned during the early hours. Soon afterward, the looting began. The rage and violence worsened when rioters began pulling passing motorists from their cars and beating them. It is unclear whether the police could have

People took to the streets immediately, focusing their rage and inciting one another to violence.

contained the riots at this stage. In any event, they did not try. Gates was away at a fund-raiser during the first riots, and it was unclear who was in charge. Police reinforcements, while available, were not called in to break up the riots for hours. The rioters seemed to realize they weren't being challenged, and the violence began to spread.

"With the Watts riots in 1965, it built and built, and on the third day the city went mad," Police Commander Robert Gil explained just after the 1992 riot. "This was completely different. The city went wild in just an hour and a half."

Looting

Looting was a central part of the riots. And as with the Watts riots twenty-five years earlier, the disturbances brought outsiders into the troubled neighborhoods to take advantage of the disorder. Yet there were some significant differences between the looting of Watts and that of 1992.

In the 1992 riots, many people caused destruction largely in their own neighborhoods, looting and burning stores within sight of their homes. In comparison, twenty-five years ago, approximately 80 percent of the looters in Watts came from outside the area. Admittedly, the 1992 destruction wasn't limited to the ghettos. Yet most of the damage occurred in South Central Los Angeles. And it was committed largely by the people who lived there. Some observers explained that this pattern showed that local residents no longer had any interest in protecting their neighborhoods.

In 1992, there was also a difference with respect to the kind of people who looted. During the Watts riots, the battle was both political and economic. It led to blacks facing off against whites and often seeking out white-owned businesses as targets of destruction. In 1992, the looters were not exclusively or even predominantly black. Because these areas were mainly Latino, large numbers of Hispanics also took part in looting, along with Asians and whites. Police arrest records during the riots show the multiracial nature of the participants. Just over seven thousand people were arrested in connection with riots on such charges as looting, assault, and breaking the city's curfew. About 13 percent were white, 50 percent were Hispanic, and 36 percent were black. There were reports, too, that the looters were not all poor and that many middle-class residents also took advantage of the disorder to steal. These statistics seemed to show a cause-and-effect relation-ship between urban unrest and increased street crime. For many, it appeared, the Rodney King verdict was less a political outrage than it was a perfect opportunity to commit serious crimes under the guise of social protest.

The rioters also seemed unconcerned with who owned the businesses they attacked and looted. The one distinct ethnic clash seemed to occur when black and Hispanic rioters confronted Asians, particularly Koreans. There were widespread reports that Korean-owned stores were being targeted by rioters. With police protection at a minimal level in the first hours of the riots, many Korean store owners banded together and armed themselves to protect their property.

In the aftermath of the Rodney King verdict, widespread looting of L.A. businesses occurred.

Churches and civic leaders tried to gather people in the area for peaceful demonstrations. Yet the riots could not be quelled. By 10 P.M. on the first day, less than seven hours after the verdict was reached, twenty-five blocks in the south central section of the city were being consumed by fire, and the impact of the riot was beginning to extend

Parts of Los Angeles burned and smoked for days. The chaos and confusion also gave rise to continued looting and random violence.

out of the ghettos. Fans leaving a Lakers basketball game that night could hear gunfire and smell smoke.

The next morning brought new trouble. Public transportation in many parts of the city shut down, and schools and many offices and stores were closed. An estimated 4,000 fires were raging, and the smoke became so dense that Los Angeles International Airport was partly shut down.

At the start of the second day, South Central Los Angeles was a war zone. Now, however, fires, looting, and robberies began spreading to wealthier communities—the predominantly white neighborhoods of Westwood, Hollywood, and Beverly Hills. Fear that the violence couldn't be contained now spread through the entire city. The roles played by the city's estimated one thousand gangs also became apparent. When the police presence faded in the first few hours, gangs from all over the area began to organize looting runs throughout the south central area. These gangs saw the chaos of urban unrest as a perfect setting for heightened street crime and violence. Their access to automatic weapons also helped to raise the level of violence and probably led to random sniping.

Police Response

In the weeks that followed the disturbances, the police were sharply criticized for not controlling the violence. There were several main reasons for the apparent breakdown. One was the absence of Chief Gates during the first crucial hours. Even though he knew he would be hard to reach on the night of the verdict, Gates had not set up a chain of command or appointed anyone to be in charge of marshaling the city's forces in the event of disturbances. When the police began to mobilize, there

The L.A.P.D. was criticized for not responding quickly or effectively to the crisis in the city.

Television

As far back as the Boston Massacre, the press has been on hand to report about disturbances in our cities. Until the late twentieth century, however, the news of these riots came by way of newspapers. Today, television is the dominant medium. It is difficult to appreciate or understand how different a world without television, with its instant communication, is. Two hundred years ago, for example, news of the capture of Bastille Prison took weeks to spread through France. In comparison, within seconds of the King verdict, television began to flash images of angry crowds of demonstrators around the city of Los Angeles and the world. As the violence grew, television coverage increased. The impact of these images raised an important question. Was television simply reporting the news or encouraging riots? This question is difficult to answer.

Los Angeles television stations spent much more air time on the images of the riots than did network television. Local coverage, in fact, was virtually nonstop for much of the rioting. Local politicians and civic leaders questioned whether showing the destruction and identifying specific locations helped to fan the flames and actually tell would-be rioters where to go. There was also a general questioning of whether television and the press gave an accurate picture of the violence by making it seem as though the entire city was in flames, when, in reality, only certain neighborhoods were burning.

Journalists and television executives countered these charges by noting they reported what was happening and that it was their job to present the worst of the violence because that was most important. Television did not fan the flames and fires that ripped through the city, they contended. It simply held a mirror up to the image so that the rest of the country could see what was happening.

Nonetheless, fearing that the coverage was inflaming the situation, Mayor Tom Bradley asked one of Los Angeles's local stations to return to some regular programming by the second night of the riots to help foster the notion that the city was getting back to normal. The station agreed, showing, as scheduled, the last episode of "The Cosby Show."

Television presented brutal images in Los Angeles. A videotape of a white trucker being beaten by local residents brought racial hatred into America's living rooms for days on end.

were complaints that they did not act aggressively. Police officials answered these complaints by saying they simply did not have the adequate numbers of officers needed to quell the riots.

In any event, by midnight of the first day of rioting, Gates admitted that the riots were not under control. California governor Pete Wilson responded by sending in 750 highway patrolmen to aid the force. In addition, he ordered two thousand National Guardsmen to the scene. Later, President Bush would send in even more troops. Eventually, over ten thousand officers and troops took to the streets to control the violence.

The Community Response

Within hours of the first disturbances, civic, social, and church leaders rallied together to try to calm the city. Mayor Bradley, however, like many politicians, found himself in a difficult position. While he said he identified with the frustrations of the black community, he was also ultimately responsible for maintaining order in the city. As the violence increased, Bradley's tolerance waned. "Don't break the law, or we will put you in jail," he warned.

It is debatable whether the rioters, black or otherwise, were willing to listen to anyone. A rally at the First African Methodist Episcopal Church within hours of the verdict on Wednesday led to a confrontation between different generations of blacks. Younger blacks argued that the time for talk had passed and that rioting would at least allow them to vent their frustration. The rift in the community and the apparent breakdown of church authority were apparent when the 1,500 people who filed out of church that night came under fire from snipers in their own neighborhood.

This led one black leader to report, "Nobody can talk to the people in the streets. Black people are shooting at

black people. The only thing they are going to understand is a show of force. I hope it's a measured show of
force."

Even as the situation grew worse, some leaders took to
the streets. Edward James Olmos, a Hispanic actor, was
visible almost immediately and tried to talk young people
out of looting. He also warned that the National Guard
might be able to stop the riots initially, but that the show
of force might bring about riots throughout the following
summer.

Ultimately, it was Rodney King who may have offered
the most moving appeal to the public. As the violence
heightened, King, in his first statement since the acquittal
of the white officers, appealed to everyone to "stop making it horrible." In an emotional plea, he ended by saying,
"People, I just want to say, you know, can we all get
along? I mean we're all stuck here for a while. Let's try to
work it out."

During the riots, Rodney King
made his first public statement since his beating to plead
for peace in South Central
Los Angeles.

The Damage

Figuring the cost of the L.A. riots was difficult. It could
not be tallied in terms of damaged or stolen property or
lost lives and mangled bodies. There was also a cost in
terms of lost opportunities and neighborhoods. And there
was the price of the new damage done to the already
fragile relations among various ethnic groups. There was
also a cost in terms of the lost trust between police and the
people of the city they protect. And, on a larger scale,
there was the price of the damage done to the image of
the United States in the world community.

The German newspaper *Mitteldeutsche Zeitung* wrote,
"In America's cities, a social time bomb is exploding. The
boom in the '80s benefited only the rich. Over 33 million
U.S. citizens, 13 percent of the population, are considered
impoverished. In the ghettos of the big cities a generation
is growing up that can expect hardly any support from
welfare in the future."

Opposite:
The destruction caused by
the riots left many without
homes and without hope.
According to some estimates,
almost one billion dollars
worth of property was
destroyed.

In Japan, the impression seemed even worse. "The Los Angeles jury could not have done more damage to their country's image abroad if they had tried," wrote the *Japan Times*.

And finally there was the cost in terms of the lost self-respect that comes when honest people of all ethnic backgrounds abandon the system and become criminals.

In the simplest terms, the L.A. riots were the worst urban disturbances in the United States in twenty-five years. The four days of violence left fifty-two people dead, mostly minorities from the inner city. There were also approximately 2,000 people hurt.

Although most major U.S. cities, such as Chicago, Boston, and New York, managed to avoid rioting and large-scale disruptions, some violence did spread to other cities. Demonstrators in San Francisco closed the

An exhausted firefighter collapses after battling one of the city's blazes.

A firefighter douses flames inside a Hispanic-owned store in Koreatown. Over 4,000 businesses reported damage from the riots.

San Francisco–Oakland Bay Bridge, while looters broke into stores on Market Street. In Las Vegas, one person was killed, and the National Guard had to be called in to restore order. Violence also erupted in Madison, Wisconsin, and Toronto, Canada. In Atlanta, peaceful demonstrations turned ugly as several hundred people began smashing store windows in the downtown area and assaulting black and white people who happened upon the fray.

Chapter 4

The Aftermath

In less than four days, peace began to return to the frightened and shaken city of Los Angeles. Police and National Guard troops reclaimed the streets. The last of the fires died, and the streets were cleared. Schools, businesses, and ballparks reopened.

City officials estimated that at least 3,500 businesses had been destroyed during the riots, the vast majority of them in the ghettos. These businesses included everything from large supermarkets, drug stores, and appliance outlets to small candy shops. Before the riots, South Central Los Angeles already had fewer stores per resident than any other section of the city. As a result of the destruction, the people's choices were limited even further.

And the prospects for rebuilding seemed bleaker than ever. Many businesspeople who suffered damage faced little chance of reclaiming their stores. A large majority had been operating without business insurance and had no way to compensate for a loss. "This is crippling, just crippling," said Gene Hale, president of the African-American Chamber of Commerce. "The insurance rates are so high that people can't afford it. Many of them will simply not be able to rebuild."

> Although the damage to property was extensive, the greatest cost was felt in human despair.

Opposite:
A National Guardsman watches over part of the neighborhood in South Central Los Angeles.

The Political Response

The riots shocked the country. Television brought home a stream of horrible and confusing images. There was sympathy for the poor and widespread astonishment over the acquittal of the police officers. Yet many people could not condone the violence. Pressure from all regions of the country to correct the injustice of the trial mounted by the day.

President Bush spoke out against the rioting soon after the violence began. Later, he toured the devastated areas of Los Angeles.

The American people looked to their political leaders for explanations and solutions. The first answers they received did not necessarily ease their fears. The uproar came at the onset of a presidential campaign and involved the incumbent president, George Bush; the Democratic nominee, Arkansas governor Bill Clinton; and independent candidates, Pat Buchanan and Ross Perot.

Responding to an explosive situation like a riot is not easy under any circumstances. In the middle of the campaign, it was even more trying for the candidates, who wanted to walk the fine line between strength and compassion. They wanted to assure the country's middle class that no matter what the reasons for the riots, they would work to restore law and order. At the same time, they wanted to assure the country's minorities and poor that they understood their frustrations.

This political tightrope walk was illustrated by the president's first comments. In the forty-eight hours after the riots began, President Bush issued eight statements, all of which condemned the violence. Many people felt that Bush did little at first to address the frustrations that led to the riot. Late on Friday, two days after the rioting began, the president tried to answer these other questions by meeting with black and other minority leaders and announcing that he found the King beating revolting. He also ordered federal officials to investigate whether charges of civil rights violations might be brought against the police officers who beat King.

Months later, federal authorities followed through on the president's pledge to investigate whether the four officers involved in the Rodney King beating had committed any federal offenses. In August, that investigation led to the charges that the four officers had violated King's civil rights by harming him while under arrest. To prove their case, federal prosecutors needed to show that the officers had deliberately hurt King, effectively punishing him before he was convicted of any crime.

Bill Clinton at first noted that the acquittal showed the "system is broken" and no longer works for minorities. However, as the violence escalated, Clinton's emphasis seemed to change. He became less concerned with the problems that caused the riots and began stressing the need to end the destruction.

Perot, for his part, condemned both the violence and the acquittal, but ultimately took a low profile. Buchanan, the most conservative of the group, was the only candidate to take a steady line. He condemned the violence and called for immediate order, a high police profile, and an end to free spending on social programs.

The pressures of the campaign became apparent when Bush and Clinton began to take swipes at each other. Bush and his Republican allies blamed the ineffective social programs of past Democratic administrations for the riots. Clinton charged that the riots sprang from frustrations caused by Republican cutbacks in aid to the poor.

Other leaders also spoke on the riots, their cause, and what the violence was saying about the state of the country's cities.

"We have to use these events as a pretext for rather dramatic action," urged Senator Bill Bradley of New Jersey. "We need honesty and straight talk. Go home tonight and reread the Kerner Commission report. And ask yourself what it is we've managed to do in all the years since it was written. The answer is: Not nearly enough."

Tom McClintock, a California state legislator, noted the riots were as much about economics as police brutality. "It is difficult to separate the social from the economic issues. Particularly in California, as the economy implodes, those at the lower rungs of the social-economic scale are feeling the pain the greatest, and it is difficult to separate those emotions from social developments."

Martin Luther III, a Fulton County, California, commissioner, said the riots should help to mobilize the nation's black communities and spur economic boycotts

Housing and Urban Development secretary Jack Kemp toured the ravaged neighborhoods of Los Angeles and pushed for new programs to improve the area.

and political activity. "When we affect white America in the pocketbook, it has always responded."

Brenda J. Muhammad, the president of a national organization known as Mothers of Murdered Sons, stressed that the verdict and riots reflect much deeper problems. "We can't trust the police, and we can't trust each other. Last year we lost more than twenty-five thousand people on the streets of America. Of that twenty-five thousand, more than 70 percent were blacks who were killed by other blacks. When are we going to raise up our arms about that?"

A Need for Programs

Talk was not enough. The American people demanded action. In the weeks that followed the riots, Republicans and Democrats began to put together plans for new urban-renewal programs. All of this came against the background of the presidential campaign, which made it difficult to determine if these ideas were practical or just designed to appeal to voters. Some of the components of both party's plans had been around for years, receiving various levels of financial and political support. In addition, there was much in common between what the Democrats and Republicans offered.

Despite these various plans, it seemed unlikely that the United States would develop a sweeping program such as President Johnson's Great Society, which cost millions of dollars. In many respects—and for a number of reasons, including tough economic times—Americans appeared to be reluctant to fund such a massive effort. In addition, there were growing questions about whether the problems of crime, poverty, drugs, and family breakdown would be solved by more expensive programs or whether the issue was really better programs.

The Republican Approach

The Republicans maintained that social issues could not be solved by massive government spending. They pointed to the fact that conditions in the inner cities have actually worsened in recent years, despite the country's increased spending on social programs—$220 billion a year, or $6,500 for every poor man, woman, and child. Some of these older programs, especially those dealing with pre-school education and public-health care, were leftovers from the Great Society program of the 1960s. They were viewed as working well, and they continue to receive support.

Yet many of the ideas offered just before and after the riots were distinctly different from the programs of the past. The Republicans promoted economic and market incentives to rebuild the inner cities and make the poor more self-sufficient. The approach was developed during the late 1980s, primarily by Housing and Urban Development secretary Jack Kemp. Some of the incentives were in place before the riots. Others had not received financial or political support. After Los Angeles, they all took on new importance.

The Republican plan included:
- HOME OWNERSHIP: Allowing tenants who live in public-housing developments to purchase the units that they are renting.
- TAX INCENTIVES: Providing tax breaks for the owners of businesses located in inner-city "enterprise zones."
- "WEED AND SEED": Establishing a two-part program designed to weed out criminals from the inner city through massive sweeps by law-enforcement agencies. This would be followed up with ongoing police efforts and social programs to provide youth-recreation programs, drug-treatment centers, and job-training efforts.
- WELFARE REFORM: Shifting welfare benefits to create monetary or benefit incentives for women with children to marry, retain their family structure, and go back to work.
- EDUCATION REFORM: Creating free-market competition between schools by allowing parents to choose the schools within a district that they want their children to attend.
- JOBS: Hiring the poor, at least temporarily, for public-service jobs.

The Plan from the Democrats

While some Democrats in Congress moved to develop their own urban-renewal plans, the most significant program was put together by Bill Clinton. In many ways, his ideas mirrored the Republican efforts:

- URBAN REINVESTMENT: Providing tax incentives and "enterprise zones" to bring jobs back to the cities and developing a plan to implement tenant-owned public housing.

As the Democratic candidate for president, Bill Clinton announced his plans for urban renewal after the L.A. riots.

- POVERTY "INSURANCE": Giving an earned-income-tax credit to ensure that no one who works full time falls below the poverty line.
- GHETTO DEVELOPMENT: Promoting the establishment of community financial institutions to provide funds for developing the ghettos.
- WELFARE REFORM: Establishing a program to reduce benefits for people who do not work.
- OTHER ELEMENTS: Developing ways to provide drug treatment on demand, a college education for those who are willing to work to pay for it through community service, apprentice training for those who skip college, tighter controls to make sure fathers pay for child support, and more police officers on foot patrol to reduce street crime.

Despite these plans, the U.S. economy tended to over-shadow urban issues throughout the election campaign.

Chapter 5

Healing the Wounds

he riots in Los Angeles—and elsewhere—undoubtedly awakened America to the problems in its inner cities. They also served notice that, while the violence and fires on the streets of Los Angeles had died out, riots might erupt in any one of the nation's ghettos. All that might be needed was a match, like the Rodney King beating.

On the positive side, the reawakening helped to stir new interest in urban problems and led to initiatives to deal with them. Ultimately, the crisis may mobilize the nation's will, which is a key to bringing about change. Yet it is difficult to imagine any single program or national policy totally wiping away the causes of urban unrest. It will always be a part of the American culture. There are no simple solutions to poverty, racial discord, and social injustice.

Racism and other social problems are deeply imbedded in the fabric of the nation. Federal and local laws have been enacted in the last thirty years to combat these problems. But their impact is limited. Laws, in effect, cannot change the way people think. At best, a law can only control the way people act.

Massive funding is not always the answer, although money is obviously needed at all government levels to put

> The riots reawakened people to America's urban problems and started the country on the road to change.

Opposite:
Willie Williams was sworn in as Los Angeles's new police chief in June 1992. Williams promised to improve relations between citizens and police.

programs into place. The cost of the Great Society ran into hundreds of millions of dollars. Reforms were made, and living conditions were improved for many Americans, but problems remained.

Poverty, racism, and a lack of adequate education, health care, and social services still plague millions of urban Americans.

To make matters worse, the problems facing American cities are greater today than ever. Poverty has reached new heights; drug addiction is rampant; gangs are more prevalent and violent; local, well-paying jobs are scarce; traditional families are harder to find; and churches and other social-support groups seem to have broken down. Against all this, the people who live in these areas are becoming increasingly hopeless and feel left out of society. Too often they no longer believe they can improve their lives or have a stake in their communities.

Admittedly, the problems facing the inner cities are complex and intimidating. It seems they can overwhelm the best attempts at dealing with them.

Beyond that, federal urban-renewal programs usually get a boost only immediately following civil disturbances, when the country's attention is focused on the problems. As the images of rioting fade, so does the political will to enact legislation to deal with them.

Often this happens because the people most in need of help, the poor, are not politically active or organized. It is difficult for them to command the respect from local or national political leaders needed to push through reforms. They are often left having others argue on their behalf. Unfortunately for the poor, politicians usually have many people to satisfy from different social and economic back-grounds. The demands of the poor have to be measured against the demands of more well-to-do voters, who may not have the same commitment to social reforms.

The other major obstacle facing the country is whether there are federal funds available to pay for a national effort

Ueberroth and Bakewell: Rebuilding Los Angeles

While the problem of rebuilding Los Angeles may be overwhelming to some, several groups moved quickly within weeks of the riots to begin restoring the devastated areas.

Two of the most prominent groups include Rebuild Los Angeles and Los Angeles's Brotherhood Crusade. These two groups have somewhat different approaches to rebuilding the city, but they are united in that they are doing more than just talking.

Rebuild Los Angeles is headed by Peter Ueberroth, former baseball commissioner and head of the L. A. Olympic Committee. Ueberroth's group has been working to encourage major corporations and financial institutions to reinvest in the troubled areas. As part of the effort, Ueberroth is using his popular public image to push hard for government legislation that would provide financial incentives, perhaps tax breaks, to any organization willing to set up shop or finance new businesses in the ghettos.

The commission, though effective in many ways, was also criticized for a number of shortcomings. Some of the most vocal criticism came from the Hispanic community, which was troubled by its lack of proportional representation on the board of directors. Of the sixty-seven directors, only sixteen were Hispanic.

Los Angeles's Brotherhood Crusade, headed by black activist and entrepreneur Danny Bakewell, is also committed to rebuilding the area's economic base. Bakewell, however, is taking a different approach. He is working hard to make sure that minority contractors and businesses, as well as individuals, receive a fair share of the riot-related demolition and construction work. In addition, Bakewell and other black leaders are trying to get minority-owned financial institutions to become directly involved with financing the rebuilding.

It will take several years before anyone can judge whether these efforts have had any long-term impact. Yet the fact that people such as Ueberroth and Bakewell began doing something constructive almost immediately provides more than good words, which were being tossed around the city following the fires and violence.

In 1992, California governor Pete Wilson (left), L.A. mayor Tom Bradley (center), and Peter Ueberroth (right) joined together to announce plans for programs to rebuild Los Angeles.

to rebuild the cities. As the riots in Los Angeles raged, most Americans believed that the greatest challenge facing the country was the economy, not the problems in the inner cities. Few realized that the problems are interconnected. The federal government was already spending about $300 billion more a year than it took in. Many people believed that until this deficit was reduced, either through cutbacks in programs or increased taxes, it would be impossible to pump substantially more money into combating the problems of the inner cities.

Opportunities

While obstacles exist, there are opportunities to improve life in the inner cities. Any improvements, however, probably will come through a mixture of government programs, social efforts, and changes in personal attitudes.

In a survey taken in the days following the disturbances, 75 percent of the people who were polled said that they would even be willing to pay higher taxes to support new social programs. However, the type of social programs they want funded has changed. The public is reluctant to see programs developed that are "giveaways," where the poor, minorities, or underprivileged get aid without making some sort of commitment in return. This new focus is one reason that there is less support today for hiring quotas, unrestricted welfare, and experimental programs that are aimed at helping people without making them self-sufficient.

As a result, any urban-renewal policy will be viewed against the efforts of the 1960s. Politicians and voters will ask the question: What has worked and what has failed?

There is also a growing consensus that social reform depends on the economic renewal of the inner cities. This means that businesses would have to return to the inner cities to provide jobs and community stability. Both major political parties support this notion and plan to

Soon after the riots, local residents took to the streets with shovels and brooms in an effort to reclaim their neighborhood.

attempt to draw businesses back to the inner cities through economic incentives.

Other efforts will also have to be made in terms of improving community relations, reestablishing trust between minorities and the police, and making inner-city residents believe that the political system can indeed work for them.

In some cities, such as Houston, Texas, and New York City, the police have attempted to improve community relations and reduce street crime by putting more officers on foot patrol. Black and other minority leaders are also in the midst of renewing an old effort to increase the political involvement of their groups by encouraging voter-registration drives and promoting members of minority groups to run for public office.

A New Chief and an Official Report

Changes have already taken place that appear to be easing tensions in the racially divided city. In June 1992, the appointment of Willie Williams, the former Philadelphia police commissioner, to replace controversial L.A. police chief Daryl Gates showed residents that the city was entering a new era.

Admittedly, Williams, a black man, hasn't had an easy time since taking the job. He has met some resistance from department members, and the L.A.P.D. has been hit with new allegations of brutality and corruption.

Yet he appeared to be making progress in restoring department morale, in part by calling for the hiring of 1,000 new officers. In addition, he succeeded in rebuilding the department's damaged image by taking a high profile in the city's various ethnic neighborhoods.

In late October 1992, an official investigative report about the riots was made public. The report, published by a panel headed by former FBI and CIA chief William Webster, severely criticized the city's leadership for failing miserably in dealing with the riots. The 222-page document blasted Daryl Gates for "failing to provide a real plan and meaningful training to control the disorder." The report also said that "Gates had a responsibility to protect...citizens. There was too little help and it came too late." Webster faulted Mayor Tom Bradley for allowing poor relations to develop between the mayor's office and the police department, which eroded the quality of police protection afforded the city of Los Angeles.

The Webster report also issued a number of recommendations for improvements in the police department. The report recommended the following:

L.A. police chief Daryl Gates was harshly criticized for failing to have a plan of response for the rioting. He was also reprimanded for allowing the violence to continue for so long.

•Increase police patrols; only 4 percent of the city's officers patrolled the city streets before the riots.

•Improve emergency communications systems, including 911.

•Have a riot-response plan developed before potentially explosive trials end.

•Improve coordination and cooperation among city officials, especially between the mayor's office and the police department.

Mayor Bradley ordered all city officials to follow the report's recommendations and accepted some of the blame for the city's poor response to the riots.

Many analysts believe that improvements can come about only if reforms meet two general goals. They must first make sure that the basic needs of the poor are met, which means providing adequate housing, education, and health care. But the work cannot stop here. The poor must also be given the chance to reclaim their self-respect, a feeling that they can control their lives and improve their economic and social conditions for themselves and their children. Meeting the first aim without considering the second will only provide the chance for new outbreaks of violence and rioting, whether in the next week or the next decade. It will also undermine the investment of time and money that has already gone into the attempts to rebuild our cities.

Against the riots and mounting problems, Roy Innis, chairman of the Congress of Racial Equality, offered some hope:

"I don't believe that this one incident—the beating of Rodney King in Los Angeles and the miscarriage of justice in Simi Valley—will turn back the real social revolution that we should be so proud of, a revolution greater than the French Revolution in the eighteenth century or the Russian Revolution at the beginning of this century. I'm convinced that the romance America had with overt racism is over."

Chronology

March 3, 1991   Rodney King is beaten by four white police officers who allege that King resisted arrest. The incident is captured on videotape by a local resident and is later aired on national television. The nation and the world express outrage and shock.

March 1992   The four police officers go on trial for the assault of Rodney King. There is controversy over the site of the trial, Simi Valley, a predominantly white area, and the lack of African Americans on the jury. The trial lasts twenty-nine days.

April 29, 1992   The four police officers, Ted Briseno, Stacey Koon, Laurence Powell, and Timothy Wind, are found not guilty. Within hours, violence erupts in Los Angeles.

April 30, 1992   Fires, looting, and violence continue to spread. Public transportation in many parts of Los Angeles is shut down, as are many schools and businesses.

May 2, 1992   Four days of violence end, leaving fifty-two people dead, thousands injured, and millions of dollars in property damage.

June 1992   Willie Williams is sworn in as chief of police, replacing Daryl Gates. He promises to improve relations between citizens and police.

August 1992   Federal authorities charge that the four police officers violated Rodney King's civil rights by harming him while under arrest.

October 1992   An official investigative report about the riots is made public, criticizing the city's leadership and recommending improvements in the police department.

For Further Reading

Barden, R. *Gangs*. Vero Beach, FL: Rourke Publishing, 1990.

Davis, Bertha. *America's Housing Crisis*. New York: Franklin Watts, 1990.

McCuen, Gary E., ed. *Inner-City Violence*. Hudson, WI: Gem Publications, 1989.

McKissak, Patricia and Frederick. *Taking a Stand Against Racism and Racial Discrimination*. New York: Franklin Watts, 1990.

Pascoe, Elaine. *Racial Prejudice*. New York: Franklin Watts, 1985.

Stewart, G. *Los Angeles*. Vero Beach, FL: Rourke Publishing, 1989.

Index

African-American Chamber of Commerce, 43
Atlanta, 17, 41

Bakewell, Danny, 55
Bastille Prison, 11, 36
Beverly Hills, 35
Boston, 40
Boston Massacre, 13, 36
Bradley, Bill, 46
Bradley, Tom, 27, 36, 37, 55, 56, 58, 60
Briseno, Ted, 28
Brotherhood Crusade, 55
Buchanan, Pat, 45, 46
Bush, George, 37, 44, 45

Carter, Jimmy, 21
Chicago, 13, 16, 17, 40
Chrysler, 23
Civil War, 14
Civil War draft riots
    dead in, 14
Cleveland, 16, 17
Clinton, Bill, 45, 46, 50

Communism
    end of in USSR, 11
Congress of Racial Equality, 60
Corono, Bert, 9

Detroit, 16, 18
Drug use, 18

Economic recession
    effect on inner cities, 23

Firestone, 23
First African Methodist
    Episcopal Church, 37
French Revolution, 11, 60

Gang warfare, 18, 24–25
Garcia, Lucrecia, 9
Gates, Daryl, 26, 31, 32, 35, 37, 58, 59
Gil, Robert, 32
Goodyear, 23
Gorbachev, Mikhail, 11
Great Depression, 19
Great Society, 20, 21, 48, 49, 54

Griego, Linda, 8

Hale, Gene, 43
Haymarket Square riot, 13–15
Hermandad Mexicana Nacional, 9
Hollywood, 35
Homelessness, 18, 24
Houston, Texas, 57

Innis, Roy, 60

Japan Times, 40
Johnson, Lyndon, 20, 48

Kemp, Jack, 47, 49
Kennedy, John F., 20
Kerner Commission
    Report, 20, 46
King, Martin Luther, Jr.
    assassination of, 17
King, Rodney, 5, 26, 39, 45
    beating, 27, 28, 29, 45, 53, 60
    federal investigation of, 45
    jury make up, 29

trial, 5, 29
verdict, 5, 10, 26, 30, 31,
    33, 36
Koon, Stacey, 28
Koreatown, 8

Las Vegas, 41
Lincoln, Abraham, 14
Los Angeles International
    Airport, 34
Los Angeles Police Department
    (L.A.P.D.), 26, 30, 35
official report on, 58
recommendations to
    improve, 58, 59
Los Angeles riots
    casualties, 6
    community response, 37, 38
    fires caused by, 4, 8, 9, 30,
        31, 33, 34, 40, 41
    impact of television on, 36,
        44
    impact on Hispanic
        businesses, 8, 9, 41, 43
    impact on Korean
        businesses, 8, 9, 33, 43
    international reaction to,
        39, 40
    looting, 33, 34, 41
    minorities and police
        tensions, 26
    police response, 35, 37
    political response, 44–51
    property loss, 6, 7, 9, 39, 43
    racial tensions, 25

Luther, Martin, III, 46

Madison, Wisconsin, 41
McClintock, Tom, 46
Mitteldeutsche Zeitung, 39
Mothers of Murdered Sons, 47
Muhammad, Brenda J., 47

National Guard, 37, 39, 43
National Rifle Association, 29
Newark, 18
New Orleans riots, 14
New York City, 16, 40, 57

Olmos, Edward James, 39
Omaha, 17

Perot, Ross, 45, 46
Powell, Laurence, 28

Rebuild Los Angeles, 55
Revolutionary War, 13
Riis, Jacob, 18, 19
Russian Revolution, 60

San Francisco, 17, 40
Simi Valley, 29, 60
Social reform, 19, 20
Social-reform proposals, 48–51
South Central Los Angeles, 8,
    23–25, 31, 34, 43
Southwest Steel, 23
Soviet Union, 11
Street crime, 18, 24

Taser guns, 27, 29
Toronto, Canada, 41
Townshend Acts, 13

Ueberroth, Peter, 55
Unión de Comerciantes
    Latinos, 9
Urban Development Action
    Grants, 21
Urban renewal, 20, 21, 48–51,
    53–56
Urban unrest
    definition of, 9, 10
    history, 11, 13–18

Ventura County, 29
Vietnam War, 20

Watts riots, 21, 32, 33
    arrests during, 17
    causes of, 16, 17
    casualties, 16, 17
    property loss, 16, 17
Webster, William, 58
Weisberg, Stanley, 28
Westwood, 35
Williams, Willie, 53, 58
Wilson, James Q., 26
    report on L.A. police, 26
Wilson, Pete, 37, 55
Wind, Timothy, 28
World War I, 15
World War II, 19, 23

Acknowledgments and photo credits

Cover: © Jean-Marc Giboux; pp. 4, 33: © Jerry Mennenga/Gamma-Liaison; pp. 6, 40, 41: Jean-Marc Giboux; pp. 7, 38: © John Barr/Gamma-Liaison; pp. 8, 10, 26, 27, 32, 34, 47, 52, 55: Wide World Photos; pp. 12, 15: North Wind Picture Archives; pp. 16, 20: AP/Wide World Photos; p. 22: © Paul S. Howell/Gamma-Liaison: pp. 24, 30, 35, 39, 57, 59: © Douglas Burrows/Gamma-Liaison; pp. 28 (left and right), 36: © Evan Agostini; p. 42: © Marc Biggins/Gamma-Liaison; p. 44: © Diana Walker/Gamma-Liaison; p. 50: © Cynthia Johnson/Gamma-Liaison.

WE THE PEOPLE

cronin

The Creek
and Their History

by Natalie M. Rosinsky

Content Adviser: Bruce Bernstein, Ph.D.,
Assistant Director for Cultural Resources,
National Museum of the American Indian, Smithsonian Institution

Reading Adviser: Rosemary G. Palmer, Ph.D.,
Department of Literacy, College of Education,
Boise State University

COMPASS POINT BOOKS
MINNEAPOLIS, MINNESOTA

Compass Point Books
3109 West 50th Street, #115
Minneapolis, MN 55410

Visit Compass Point Books on the Internet at *www.compasspointbooks.com*
or e-mail your request to *custserv@compasspointbooks.com*

On the cover: A Creek cabin scene painted by 19th-century artist
and career military officer Seth Eastman

Photographs ©: Prints Old & Rare, cover, back cover (far left), 30; Library of Congress, back cover, 32, 37;
Archives and Manuscript Division of the Oklahoma Historical Society, neg. #6393, 4; Courtesy of U.S. Army
Quartermaster Museum, Fort Lee, Virginia, 5; Corbis, 6, 22, 36; Smithsonian American Art Museum,
Washington, D.C./Art Resource, N.Y., 7; MPI/Getty Images, 9, 21, 26, 33; Marilyn "Angel" Wynn, 12, 13, 15,
18, 39, 41; EyeWire, 16; North Wind Picture Archives, 19, 20, 27, 28, 29; From the original painting by Mort
Kunstler, "Green Corn Ceremony of the Creek" c1976 Mort Kunstler, Inc., 24; Smithsonian American Art
Museum, Gift of Mrs. Joseph Harrison Jr., 25; The Granger Collection, New York, 31; White House
Collection, courtesy White House Historical Association, 34; Woolaroc Museum, 35; Kit Breen, 38, 40.

Creative Director: Terri Foley
Managing Editor: Catherine Neitge
Art Director: Keith Griffin
Photo Researcher: Marcie C. Spence
Designer/Page production: Bradfordesign, Inc./Bobbie Nuytten
Cartographer: XNR Productions, Inc.
Educational Consultant: Diane Smolinski

Library of Congress Cataloging-in-Publication Data
Rosinsky, Natalie M. (Natalie Myra)
  The Creek and their history / by Natalie M. Rosinsky.
     p. cm.—(We the people)
  Includes bibliographical references and index.
  ISBN 0-7565-0836-3 (hardcover : alk. paper)
1. Creek Indians—History—Juvenile literature. 2. Creek Indians—Social life and customs—Juvenile
literature. I. Title. II. We the people (Series) (Compass Point Books)
  E99.C9R67 2005
  975.004'97385—dc22   2004019002

TABLE OF CONTENTS

Forced from Their Homes 4

Who Are the Creek? 8

In Summer and Winter 12

Family, Clan, and Village 16

At Home 20

Respecting the Spirits 22

Peace Leaders and War Leaders 25

Allies and Enemies 27

"Land . . . I Am Never to Look Upon Again" . . . 31

Survival and Growth 38

Glossary 42

Did You Know? 43

Important Dates 44

Important People 45

Want to Know More? 46

Index 48

FORCED FROM THEIR HOMES

On a hot July day in 1837, citizens in the port city of Montgomery, Alabama, witnessed a terrible sight. The defeated Creek Indians were being forced from their homes. They had been rounded up by an army of 11,000 men. The 2,500 Creek soon would board steamboats to take them far away, to the western Indian Territory that today is Oklahoma. Their long journey would include forced marches as well as river travel.

Many Native Americans made the long, difficult journey to Indian Territory.

There were only 800 warriors among them. They and their leader, the 84-year-old Chief Eneah Emathla, trudged toward Montgomery wearing heavy iron chains. As one observer later said, "Old Eneah Emathla marched all the way, handcuffed and chained like the others. He never uttered a complaint." Yet the mood of the defeated Creek was so grim that one warrior cut his own throat as they entered Montgomery. Another warrior, knowing the odds against him, attacked one of the guards. The Creek man killed this guard, but then he was immediately shot to death.

General Thomas Jesup captured Eneah Emathla.

5

About 1,000 of these 2,500 Creek died on their long journey westward. Disease killed many. Often, children and the elderly were the first to die. The Creek were not given time to honor their dead. A reporter wrote that these bodies were just left by the road, "covered only with brush." More than 300 Creek people also drowned when their overcrowded steamboat, piloted by a drunken crew, hit another boat and sank. Chief Eneah Emathla may have been among those who drowned.

Indians were moved west by steamboats and forced marches.

Between 1836 and the end of 1837, the U.S. government forced more than 15,000 Creek people to move from their homes in Georgia and Alabama. Disease and disaster followed them on their journey to Oklahoma and upon their arrival there. About 3,500 of these people died. As one Creek chief said soon after their arrival, "Our road had been a long one, and on it we have laid the bones of our men, women, and children."

This forced removal was a bitter period in the lives of a people with a long, proud history and many traditions.

Famous artist George Catlin painted Tel-maz-ha-za, a Creek "warrior of distinction," in 1834.

WHO ARE THE CREEK?

The Creek are a native people of the southeastern woodlands. Many historians believe that more than 10,000 years ago, the Creek's ancestors crossed a land bridge from Asia to North America. These people slowly spread eastward. They settled in what is now Alabama

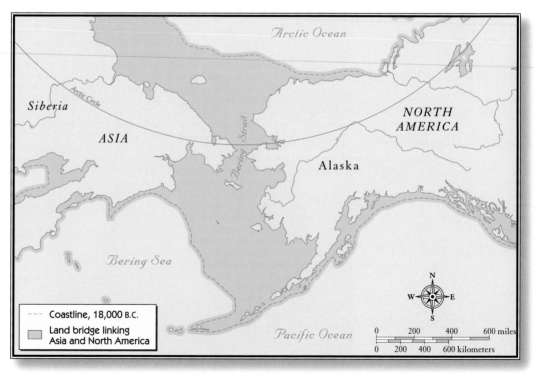

Thousands of years ago, a land bridge linked Asia and North America.

and Georgia. Some ancestors of the Creek belonged to the ancient civilizations of mound builders. Large ruins of the mound builders have been found in Ohio as well as in Mississippi and Georgia.

The Creek belonged to different tribes. These included the Muskogee, Hitchiti, Apalachee, Alabama,

The Great Serpent Mound in Adams County, Ohio, was built about 2,000 years ago.

9

and Yuchi. Most of these tribes spoke one of the Muskogean languages. It was their shared way of life and common enemies, though, that united the tribes into what is called the Creek confederacy.

In the 17th century, English colonists began using the name *Creek* after an encounter with one tribe near Ochese Creek (near present-day Macon, Georgia). The name stuck and was soon used to refer to all the tribes in this area. In their own languages, these tribes often called themselves the Muskogee (pronounced mus-KOH-gee). This word means "wet or flooded land." The many creeks, streams, and rivers in this area were important to its peoples.

The Creek often fought with two neighbor tribes, the Chickasaw and the Cherokee. When English colonists arrived in the 17th century, there were between 15,000 and 25,000 Creeks. Hardships caused by white settlers, as well as disease and wars, killed thousands of the Creek.

Today, there are about 54,000 Creek. Most live in eastern Oklahoma, which is the location of the Muscogee (Creek) Nation. About 2,000 Creek remain in Alabama, home to the Poarch Band Creek.

The Creek have reservations in Alabama and Oklahoma.

IN SUMMER AND WINTER

The Creeks were farmers who also gathered, fished, and hunted their food. Their mild climate and long growing season allowed Creek women to plant and harvest two yearly crops of corn. This important food was cooked in stews as well as baked. Creek women also grew beans,

Traditional foods include pumpkins, squash, nuts, beans, and seeds.

squash, and pumpkins. They gathered berries, nuts, seeds, other fruit, wild onions, and potatoes. Women also gathered the plants used for medicine.

Creek men used spears or bows and arrows to catch freshwater fish. They hunted deer, smaller animals such as rabbits and squirrels, and birds such as wild turkeys. Men stalking deer sometimes wore deerskins to trick these

Indian hunters wore deer capes to more easily sneak up on their prey.

13

animals. Hunters used bows and arrows, spears, traps, and blowguns. Creek men made blowguns from a plant called river cane that grows near creeks and swamps. Sharp darts made from small, thin pieces of wood were inserted into the hollowed-out tubes of the river cane.

Some foods were eaten right away, but some were dried and stored for winter months or for celebrations.

Creek farmers built permanent homes near rivers or other bodies of water. These locations made watering their crops on the nearby rich soil easier. The locations also made it easier to travel in long dugout canoes made from cypress or poplar logs. The Creek grouped their homes in *italwa*, or villages.

Men built separate summer and winter houses. To keep cool in summer, they covered wood poles with roofs made of leaves or woven grass. This kept off the hot sun while the open sides let in breezes. To keep warm in winter, Creek men built low, round houses. Thick walls made of mud and grass kept the comfortable heat of campfires inside these dark, smoky homes. Bark roofs completed these dwellings. Creek families often stored things in separate sheds.

Canoes were made from poplar logs.

FAMILY, CLAN, AND VILLAGE

Creek families were large. Besides a mother, father, and children, a home might also include grandparents, other older relatives, and young orphans. A mother's family was most important. Membership in clans passed from mothers to their children.

16

The bear is a symbol of a Creek clan.

There were nearly 50 different Creek clans. Each had its own totem creature or force of nature as its symbol. These included the Bear, Eagle, Fish, and Wind clans. The Creek believed that clan members had some of the strengths of their totem. They also felt that being loyal to other clan members was very important. A clan was held responsible for its members. Getting revenge for harm to one person or family sometimes caused fighting between clans. It also caused wars between Creeks and neighboring tribes.

Because Creek custom required people to marry outside their clans, they often married people from other villages. This strengthened ties between the villages, and helped unite them into a confederacy.

The growth of new italwa was another tie. By custom, each village held 400 to 600 people. When this limit was reached, an italwa divided into two smaller, nearby communities. These communities remained friendly.

A Creek summer home would be located in an italwa, or village.

Large italwa were all arranged in the same way. In the center, they had a large open space for important ceremonies and gatherings. These might include fiercely played ball games and other competitions. The Creek called their game of stickball "the little brother of war." They sometimes used this rough game to settle disagreements between towns. Older Creeks often played a bowling ball game called chunkey.

The Creek kept a sacred fire burning in the center plaza of the italwa. There might be a sweat lodge for ceremonies to make people pure. The plaza also held two large buildings for council meetings. The open-sided building was used in summer. In winter, the closed building kept village leaders warm. The homes of village leaders were close to the plaza. The homes of less-important people were further away, connected by trails. These trails led outward to the fields that were farmed by the women.

Creek villages were sometimes surrounded by high stake fences called palisades.

19

At Home

Besides doing the farming, women cooked food and made pots, baskets, and clothing. They used bone needles and thread made from plants to sew the deerskin skirts they wore. Men wore animal hide breechcloths and, sometimes,

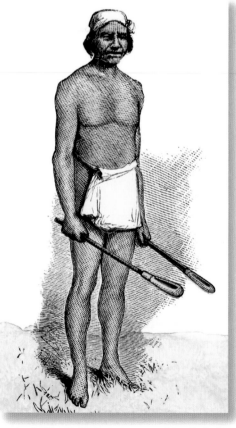

leggings. In winter, Creek people added cloaks of grass or bark to keep warm. In their mild climate, though, they usually went barefoot. Children did not wear clothes until the age of 3 or 4. For special events, the Creek wore body paint made from natural dyes. Sometimes, they tattooed themselves with these natural dyes as well.

An Indian ballplayer wears a breechcloth.

An 1844 hand-colored lithograph of Mistipee, a Creek boy holding his bow and arrows

Women took care of babies, often keeping them safe in cradleboards. They raised children until the age of 3 or 4. Boys then began to learn skills from their mother's male relatives. They practiced archery, wrestling, and throwing to become successful warriors. They learned to hunt and fish. Fathers, in turn, trained their own sisters' sons. Girls stayed with their mothers and female relatives to learn their jobs. Men's and women's work were kept separate. Even though women owned the fields and houses, men cleared the land and built Creek homes. They made weapons for war as well as hunting.

RESPECTING THE SPIRITS

Stories told by relatives taught Creek children about their world, their past, and their people's beliefs. The Creeks believed in many gods and spirits. One main god, they said, had created this world and the first members of each Creek clan. It was now their duty to bring honor to their clans and keep balance in the world.

The Creek respect the spirit of all living things, like the eagle, which is a clan symbol.

Respecting the spirits inside all living things helped keep this balance. Before gathering food, Creek women thanked spirits of the earth. Before hunting, Creek men thanked spirits of the creatures they tracked. Their medicine man was the valued leader who taught them the correct ways to pray and complete other ceremonies. He also helped heal the sick.

Summer harvest was when the Creek held their most important celebration, the Green Corn Ceremony or *poskita*. This event lasted between four and eight days. The Creeks sang, danced, and told stories to honor corn, which they called their "grain of life." Like their mound-building ancestors, they also honored the sun, which helped corn grow. The sacred fire in their plaza was a symbol of the powerful sun. At this special time, Creek people married, forgave their enemies, and started new italwa. It was a joyful, but serious, beginning to the new year.

23

The Creek danced at the Green Corn Ceremony, or poskita.

To make themselves pure for the poskita, Creek men swallowed a dark, bitter drink that made them vomit. This custom was also followed before other important events. It began special hunts, council meetings, and battles.

PEACE LEADERS AND WAR LEADERS

The Creek had different leaders in peace and war. During peaceful times, a chief called a *mico* led each village. He was chosen by the community's best warriors and medicine men. These people formed the council of their italwa. Together, the mico and council made laws for their village. If the mico and council could not fully agree, they acted on what the majority thought best.

Sometimes, the micos of villages in an area met. Every year, each italwa sent a leader to a meeting of the whole Creek confederacy. The people there formed the council for the entire Creek nation.

A George Catlin portrait of a Creek chief, Steeh-tcha-kó-me-co

25

In times of war, a war leader called a *tustunnuggee* led Creek warriors from an italwa. He was helped by other skilled warriors who had proven themselves in battle. By tradition, italwa were called either red or white towns. Red stood for war, while white stood for peace. These names were sometimes used to identify different sides in the fierce ball games the Creek played. The Creek practiced some of their fighting skills during competitions between villages.

B Romans fecit

Characteristick head of a Creek War Chief.

A 1775 drawing of a Creek war chief wearing hoop earrings and a skullcap

When Europeans reached Creek territory, however, a series of real wars and terrible events began.

26

ALLIES AND ENEMIES

Spanish explorer Hernando de Soto reached Creek territory in 1540. Over the next two centuries, the Spanish, French, and English competed for Creek land and its rich furs. In 1670, the English established the colony of Charles Town in nearby Carolina (present-day Charleston, South Carolina). This increased European competition.

Hernando de Soto took Indian prisoners as he marched through the South.

At first, the Creek seemed to benefit from European interest in deerskin and furs. Creek leaders traded these for guns and tools. After a while, though, the Creek began to depend on these tools. They slaughtered so many deer for skins to trade that the animals became a scarce food source.

Then the Creek became involved in European wars on their land. The English and French fought the French and Indian War from 1754 to 1763. During this war, the Creek sided with the English winners. The Creek lost lives but retained much of their land. They remained allies of the English. This alliance harmed the Creek after

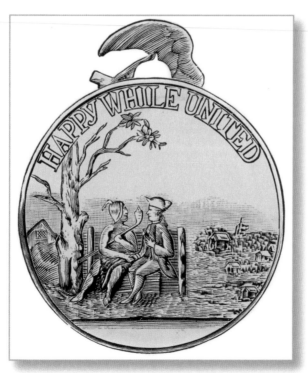

The British gave this medal to Indians who supported them during the American Revolution.

the English lost the Revolutionary War (1775-1783) with their American colonies. The new United States was now angry with the Creek.

Nonetheless, Creek leader Alexander McGillivray successfully bargained for some Creek rights in a treaty signed in 1790. The son of a Creek woman and a Scots trader and politician, McGillivray was shrewd but honest. Some native leaders had taken bribes to sign away rights. McGillivray declared that President George Washington himself could not bribe him "had he the 13 colonies in his belly" to offer.

Alexander McGillivray

At this time, money and European ways had become increasingly important to the Creek and their neighboring tribes, the Chickasaw, Choctaw, Seminole, and Cherokee. By the early 1800s, these peoples had adopted so many European customs that settlers began calling them the Five Civilized Tribes. Even though many settlers approved of their civilized behavior, the United States did not treat the Creek well. The government broke many of the promises it had made in the 1790 treaty and later agreements.

The Creek lived in cabins like this one painted by 19th-century artist and career military officer Seth Eastman.

"LAND ... I AM NEVER TO LOOK UPON AGAIN"

Ignoring the treaty, U.S. settlers began taking Creek land by force. The government even built roads through Creek territory. Tribal leaders could not agree on what to do about this. Some believed war was the answer. Their views gained strength as a popular Shawnee leader, Chief Tecumseh, also urged native peoples to fight the government.

Between 1813 and 1814, a group known as the Red Stick Creek, led by Chief Menawa, fought a larger U.S. Army

Creek armed with hatchets, bows and arrows, and rifles rush to defend their village against American soldiers during the Creek War.

31

force led by General Andrew Jackson. In this Creek War, some Cherokee warriors and and a group called the White Stick Creek helped Jackson. Chief William McIntosh was a Creek leader who helped Jackson. At the Battle of Horseshoe Bend in Alabama, Jackson and his allies defeated the Red Stick warriors. At least 800 of the 1,000 Red Stick warriors died in the battle. Jackson's forces, on the other hand, lost only about 200 of their 3,300 men.

This defeat forced some Red Stick Creek from their land. Some moved west, while others fled south to Florida. Wounded Chief Menawa voiced his people's sadness when he said, "Last night I saw the sun set for the last time, and its light shine upon the treetops and the land and the water that I am never to look upon again." Andrew Jackson, though, became famous for winning this war. This fame

Chief Menawa

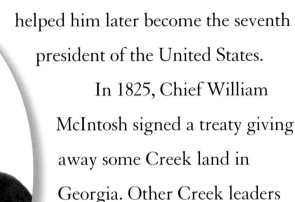

Chief William McIntosh

helped him later become the seventh president of the United States.

In 1825, Chief William McIntosh signed a treaty giving away some Creek land in Georgia. Other Creek leaders disagreed with McIntosh and felt he had broken Creek laws. They suspected he might have taken a bribe. One chief named Opothleyaholo voiced the tribe's anger when he said McIntosh had "a double snake tongue." These Creek leaders ordered McIntosh's death.

McIntosh's family later described how, in the early morning hours of April 30, 1825, more than 100 warriors surrounded the chief's house and killed him "by shooting more than 100 [bullets] into [him]." Nonetheless, the U.S. government held the Creek to the treaty McIntosh had signed. Some Creeks in Georgia had to move west.

In 1832, when Andrew Jackson was president, Creek leaders were pressured into signing more treaties. These exchanged most of their remaining traditional land for land in the western Indian Territory that later became Oklahoma. As a result, between 1836 and 1837, the U.S. Army removed between 15,000 and 20,000 Creek from their homes. It was while they were fighting against this removal that Chief Eneah Emathla and his followers were caught and taken to Montgomery.

In Indian Territory, the Creek uneasily joined their former neighbors, the Chickasaw and Choctaw peoples, who had already

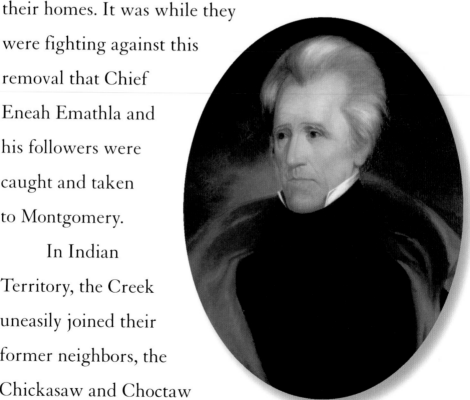

President Andrew Jackson

34

The forced march of the Cherokee in 1838 is known as the Trail of Tears.

been forced to move there. In 1838, most of their Cherokee neighbors were also forced to relocate. The journey of the Cherokee was so bitter and painful that in their own language they called it the Trail of Tears.

In Oklahoma, the Creek continued to struggle. They faced disease, hunger created by the government's failures to deliver supplies, and sometimes unfriendly neighbors. During the American Civil War of 1861 to

1865, most Creek sided with the Southern Confederate states, which lost to the Northern Union forces. A Creek regiment of soldiers was one of the last in the Confederate Army to be defeated.

During the Civil War, the Creek leader Opothleyaholo led several thousand Creek who were loyal to the Union. Escaping from Confederate forces to Kansas, Opothleyaholo led his people on a second "trail of tears." One winter, their bare feet left bloody footprints in the snow as they stumbled to keep ahead of their enemies. Yet their loyalty was not

Delegates from 34 tribes gathered at the Creek Council House in Indian Territory (Oklahoma) in 1880. The decade would bring them further loss of their land.

rewarded. In 1866, the United States punished all Creek people by taking away nearly half of their Oklahoma territory.

In 1887, the Dawes General Allotment Act further reduced the land set aside for such reservations. The Creek lost more territory in 1889, when the government opened Oklahoma to homesteaders. Traditions as well as land were lost at this time. Christian missionaries continued their efforts to convert Creek people and their neighbors.

Homesteaders raced to claim land in Oklahoma in 1889.

37

SURVIVAL AND GROWTH

In the 20th century, native peoples worked to regain their legal rights. In 1971, the Muscogee Nation in Oklahoma began electing its own officials. Today, Creek people there govern themselves. They make their own laws, carried out by an elected principal chief, assistant chief, and council members. They also have their own judges. The Poarch Band Creek in Alabama established a similar tribal government in 1984.

The Muscogee (Creek) Nation has its headquarters in Okmulgee, Oklahoma.

The Muscogee (Creek) Nation operates gambling establishments called casinos. It is using money from these to build and operate health services and develop a tribal college for its people. The Muscogee Nation is also developing construction and communication businesses. As Muscogee construction manager Pat Freeman recently said, "We've got a building boom going and … right now one of our pluses is upgrading the services to our people."

The restored Creek Council House and Museum in Okmulgee, which was built in 1880, houses an exhibit of Creek historical items and an art gallery.

A Creek man and his grandson perform a dance at a powwow.

The Poarch Band Creek in Alabama operate a casino, hotel, metal parts factory, and a farm. These provide members with money to achieve their goals, which include passing along their culture and beliefs to future generations. The Poarch Band Creek hold an annual pow-wow that draws thousands to celebrate Creek traditions.

Today, about 30,000 Creek continue to practice their traditional religion, including the Green Corn Ceremony. Some Creek honor such important customs while they also practice Christianity. The Creek language today is spoken by several thousand Muscogee and Seminole people in Oklahoma. Seminoles in Florida also speak Creek.

The Creek people have suffered great losses, including most of their traditional land. Yet they have survived and continue to grow. They look toward a future that offers all Creek people many opportunities, including the chance to honor their history and traditions.

A Creek man in traditional dress

GLOSSARY

alliance—an agreement between people or countries to help each other in times of trouble

breechcloths—short clothes that wrap around the lower part of someone's body

confederacy—a group of peoples, organizations, or countries that work together and have the same main leader

culture—the traditions and products of a group of people

reservation—a large area of land set aside for Native Americans

revenge—to harm someone or something in return for having been hurt

stalking—following quietly and secretly in order to kill or harm

sweat lodge—building in which heat causes the occupants to perspire, to purify the body and spirit

totem—an animal or natural object believed to be related in a holy way to a group of people; also the picture or statue of this animal or object

uttered—spoken out loud to other people

DID YOU KNOW?

- One of the plants the Creek used to relieve pain was willow bark. Today, it is one of the ingredients in aspirin.

- The Seminole war leader named Osceola was born into a Creek tribe. After his family lost their Alabama home in the 1813 Creek War, they and 9-year-old Osceola joined Seminole relatives in Florida.

- Place names in Georgia such as Chattahoochee and Chickamauga come from the Creek language. In Oklahoma, the community of Muskogee is named for the Creek people who moved there.

- By the 1870s, some newspaper articles and ads in Oklahoma were being written in the Creek language.

IMPORTANT DATES

Timeline

1540	Spanish explorer Hernando de Soto arrives in Creek territory
1790	Creek leader Alexander McGillivray signs a treaty with the United States
1813	Creek War ends with the Battle of Horseshoe Bend
1825	Chief William McIntosh signs away the last of Creek land in Georgia
1836	The U.S. Army forces between 15,000 and 20,000 Creek to move to Indian Territory (Oklahoma)
1866	Laws pass that take away about half of Muskogee territory in Oklahoma
1889	U.S. government opens Oklahoma territory to homesteaders
1971	Muscogee Nation elects its own leaders
1984	Poarch Band Creek in Alabama gets official recognition and reservation land

IMPORTANT PEOPLE

HERNANDO DE SOTO (1500-1542)
Spanish explorer who was among the first Europeans to meet the Creek

ENEAH EMATHLA (1753-1837)
Creek chief who led a failed revolt in 1837

ANDREW JACKSON (1767-1845)
U.S. Army general who led U.S. forces that won the "Red Stick" War against the Creek in 1813-1814; Jackson became U.S. president in 1829

ALEXANDER McGILLIVRAY (1759-1793)
Creek leader who bargained for a treaty with the new United States that let the Creek keep some traditional land

CHIEF WILLIAM McINTOSH (1775?-1825)
Creek leader who fought alongside Andrew Jackson in the Creek War of 1813-1814; McIntosh was killed by other Creek in 1825

MENAWA (1765-1843?)
Creek chief who led the "Red Stick" forces in the 1813-1814 war

OPOTHLEYAHOLO (1798?-1863)
Creek chief who led Creek loyal to the Union during the Civil War; he was one of the Creek leaders who had William McIntosh killed

WANT TO KNOW MORE?

At the Library

Bruchac, Joseph. *The Great Ball Game: A Muskogee Story.* New York: Dial Books, 1994.

Girod, Christina M. *Native Americans of the Southeast.* San Diego: Lucent Books, 2001.

Koestler-Sack, Rachel A. *Osceola, 1804-1838.* Mankato, Minn.: Blue Earth Books, 2003.

Libal, Autumn. *Creek: North American Indians of Today.* Broomall, Pa.: Mason Crest Publishers, 2003.

Smith, Cynthia Leitich. *Jingle Dancer.* New York: Morrow, 2000.

Smith, Cynthia Leitich. *Rain Is Not My Indian Name.* New York: HarperCollins, 2001.

On the Web

For more information on the *Creek,* use FactHound to track down Web sites related to this book.

1. Go to *www.facthound.com*

2. Type in a search word related to this book or this book ID: 0756508363.

3. Click on the *Fetch It* button.

Your trusty FactHound will fetch the best Web sites for you!

On the Road

Etowah Indian Mounds

813 Indian Mounds Road S.W.

Cartersville, GA 30120

770/387-3747

To see the remains of the mound builders who lived in the Southeast before the Creek and who were some of their ancestors

National Museum of the American Indian

Fourth Street and Independence Avenue Southwest

Washington, DC 20560

202/287-2020

To visit this new Smithsonian Institution museum to learn more about the Creek and other native peoples

Look for more We the People books about this era:

The Alamo

The Arapaho and Their History

The Battle of the Little Bighorn

The Buffalo Soldiers

The California Gold Rush

The Chumash and Their History

The Erie Canal

Great Women of the Old West

The Lewis and Clark Expedition

The Louisiana Purchase

The Mexican War

The Ojibwe and Their History

The Oregon Trail

The Pony Express

The Powhatan and Their History

The Santa Fe Trail

The Transcontinental Railroad

The Trail of Tears

The Wampanoag and Their History

The War of 1812

A complete list of We the People titles is available on our Web site: www.compasspointbooks.com

INDEX

Alabama, 7, 8, 11, 32, 40
ancestors, 8-9
Apalachee tribe, 9

blowguns, 14

canoes, 14
ceremonies, 18, 19, 23-24, 40
Charleston, South Carolina, 27
Cherokee tribe, 10, 30
Chickasaw tribe, 10, 30, 34-35
chiefs, 5, 6, 25, 26, 31-32, 33, 34,
    36, 38
children, 6, 16, 20, 21, 22
Choctaw tribe, 30, 34-35
Christianity, 37, 41
clans, 16-17
clothing, 20
corn, 12
cradleboards, 21
Creek confederacy, 10, 25
Creek War, 32

Dawes General Allotment Act, 37
diseases, 6, 7, 10, 35
dugout canoes, 14

families, 15, 16, 17
farming, 12-13, 14, 19, 21
fishing, 12, 13, 21

Florida, 32, 41
food, 12-13, 14, 20, 23, 28
forced removal, 4-7, 34-35

games, 18, 26
Georgia, 7, 9, 33
Green Corn Ceremony, 23, 40

Hitchiti tribe, 9
houses, 14-15, 19, 21
hunting, 12, 13-14, 21, 23

Indian Territory, 4, 34
italwa (villages), 14, 17-18, 19, 23,
    24, 25, 26

Jackson, Andrew, 32-33, 34

language, 10, 41

marriage, 17, 23
McGillivray, Alexander, 29
McIntosh, William (chief), 32, 33
medicine men, 23
men, 13-14, 20, 21, 23, 24
missionaries, 37
Mississippi, 9
mound builders, 9, 23
Muscogee (Creek) Nation, 9, 10,
    11, 38, 39, 41

Muskogean languages, 10

Oklahoma, 4, 7, 11, 34, 35, 37, 38,
    41

Poarch Band Creek, 11, 38, 40

Red Stick Creek, 31-32
religion, 22-23, 37, 40-41
reservations, 37
river cane, 14

sacred fire, 19, 23
Seminole tribe, 30, 41
settlers, 10, 27, 30, 31, 37
Shawnee tribe, 31
Spanish exploration, 27
sweat lodges, 19

totems, 17
treaties, 29, 30, 31, 33, 34

villages, 14, 17-18, 19, 23, 24, 25, 26
vomit custom, 24

wars, 10, 17, 21, 25, 26, 28-29, 31,
    32, 34-36
women, 12-13, 19, 20, 21, 23

Yuchi tribe, 10

About the Author

Natalie M. Rosinsky writes about history, social studies, economics, science, and other fun things. One of her two cats usually sits on her computer as she works in Mankato, Minnesota. Natalie earned graduate degrees from the University of Wisconsin and has been a high school and college teacher.